MAKING SCRIPTURE PERSONAL

40 Days in Romans

42 Days in I Corinthians

28 Days in II Corinthians

—Anita K. Miller

Rev 1211016.0

ISBN: 9781091812185

Dedication

To my children and future generations

Making Scripture Personal

Forward

I am hungry to personally hear the Lord speak from His Word.

Sometimes, even after years walking with Jesus, this isn't easy.

Every day brings new challenges. Busyness, unexpected interruptions, the influence of others, and concern about world events can impact my peace and distract my thinking.

Through my work counseling and leading groups, I've discovered the value of asking open-ended questions that anyone can wrestle with and apply to their own life.

Certain questions help focus my attention so that the Holy Spirit can speak directly to me through the scriptures apart from the things in my life that would otherwise distract me.

That's when scripture penetrates my heart and mind in a way I can apply immediately. I become ready to be about the things that God has called me to do. I find myself more filled with joy, hope, and all the fruit of the Spirit. I am refreshed and renewed.

As you spend time in the Word through the *Making Scripture Personal* series, I pray that the Holy Spirit encourages and refreshes your relationship with the Lord in the freedom that only comes through walking day by day with Jesus.

— *Anita K. Miller*

My purpose for reading the *Making Scripture Personal* series is:

❑ To intimately interact directly with scripture

❑ To desire more of God's Word

❑ To assess deeply my heart and mind

❑ To clarify my identity and purpose on earth

❑ To discover my connection with the Body of Christ

❑ To participate in one-on-one or group sharing

❑ To align myself with a biblical worldview as my impact increases on the world around me

❑ Other...

_____

_____

_____

_____

How to use this book

This book's format offers you the flexibility to adapt to what works best for you.

Each day covers key passages, but may not include every verse from that passage.

You may choose to read the entire passage in the version of your choice.

If you need additional room to write your thoughts than the space allows, consider using a notebook or the *Making Scripture Personal Companion Journal*.

For discussion groups

The goal of meeting as a group using this material is to have a team of people who support one another as each individual meets with the Lord through scripture.

Counseling, resolving one another's issues, and providing "here's what you need to do" responses are counterproductive to supportive group dynamics.

Great group interaction

1. Read the material ahead of time and come prepared.

2. Answer the "What was significant to me and why?" question each session.

3. Refrain from dominating the conversation.

4. Remain authentic, supportive, and confidential.

5. Pray together

40 Days
In
ROMANS

Day 1: **Romans 1:1-7**

Paul chose to follow Jesus when he was called to be an apostle of the gospel of Jesus Christ (verse 1).

❑ Paul said that through Jesus he had received grace and an apostleship for obedience to faith in Jesus' name throughout all nations (verse 5)

❑ Speaking to Christians—in this case those in Rome—Paul said they, too, were called by grace to Jesus Christ *for obedience* to the faith, and to share Christ to all nations (verses 5-6)

How has Jesus called me to follow Him and share Him with others?

_____

_____

_____

I need to know Jesus to share Him with others. Christ's nature was both flesh and Spirit.

...Jesus Christ our Lord, who was born of the seed of David according to the flesh.

—Romans 1:3

[Jesus was] declared to be the Son of God with power according to the Spirit of holiness, by the resurrection from the dead.

—Romans 1:4

How has my fleshly nature been impacted by Jesus' resurrection power and the Spirit of holiness?

_____

_____

_____

_____

_____

Day 2: **Romans 1:8-15**

Paul was a loving example of how to minister Jesus to others. Here are a few ways he displayed his love and care:

- ❑ He assured them they were loved by God (verse 7)

- ❑ He sent a blessing of grace and peace (verse 7)

- ❑ He was thankful for them (verse 8)

- ❑ He prayed for them without ceasing (verse 9)

- ❑ He sought the Lord about spending time with them (verse 10)

- ❑ He wanted to help them be rooted in Jesus (verse 11)

- ❑ He desired to gain encouragement together with them, and to encourage them in their mutual faith (verse 12)

When have I experienced this type of ministry?

_____

_____

_____

_____

_____

How can I use this model to minister to those in my life?

_____

_____

_____

_____

_____

_____

Day 3: **Romans 1:16-25**

For I am not ashamed of the gospel of Christ, for it is the power of God to salvation for everyone who believes….

—Romans 1:16

How can I display the gospel of Christ and the power of God so that others can find salvation in Jesus?

_____

_____

God's wrath is revealed from heaven against (verse 18):

- ❏ Ungodliness (verse 18)

- ❏ Unrighteousness (verse 18)

- ❏ Those who suppress truth (verse 18)

- ❏ Those who ignore the clear signs of God's attributes within us and through His creation (verse 19-20, Psalm 19:1-6)

- ❏ Those who proclaimed to know God but do not glorify Him as God (verse 21)

- ❏ Those whose minds are on futile things and their *hearts* are darkened (verse 21)

- ❏ Those who lust and dishonor their bodies (verse 24)

- ❏ Those who change truth for a lie and worship created things rather than the Creator (verse 25)

What helps my heart, mind, and behavior remain in a good place against these things?

_____

_____

_____

_____

Day 4: **Romans 1:24-28**

Paul recognized the extensive ungodliness occurring in the Roman culture. He points out some of the root issues.

When lusts of the heart take control, and created things are worshiped above the Creator, a person becomes vulnerable to:

❑ Vile passions (verse 26)

❑ Going counter to the way God designed men and women to interact with each other (verse 27)

How best do I keep my heart from being overtaken by lust?

_____

_____

_____

What helps me keep my mind on the Creator more than on what/who He created?

_____

_____

_____

Another root issue leading to ungodliness:

❑ Thinking about God has no place in their mindset (verse 28)

What helps me retain God in my thinking?

_____

_____

_____

_____

Day 5: **Romans 1:28-2:3**

...They [those who suppress the truth about God] did not like to retain God in their knowledge, God gave them over to a debased mind, to do those things which are not fitting; being filled with all unrighteousness....

—Romans 1:28-29

Failing to retain God in one's knowledge and mind results in:

- ❑ Sexual immorality, wickedness, covetousness, maliciousness; envy, murder, strife, deceit, evil-mindedness, gossip (verse 29)

- ❑ Backbiting, hating God, violence, pride, boasting, inventing evil things, disobeying one's parents (verse 30)

- ❑ Loss of having discernment, trust, love, forgiveness, and mercy (verse 31)

[Those] who, knowing the righteous judgment of God, that those who practice such things are deserving of death, not only do the same but also approve of those who practice them.

—Romans 1:32

Which of the acts listed above are not issues for me?

_____

_____

Which acts do I need God's continual help to avoid?

_____

_____

How do I avoid having a judgmental attitude toward those who practice these acts, and yet not support their sin?

_____

_____

_____

Day 6: **Romans 2:4-10**

**...[E]ternal life to those who by patient continuance in doing good...
but glory, honor, and peace to everyone who works what is good....**
—Romans 2:7, 10

...[T]he goodness of God leads us to repentance....
—Romans 2:4

How is God's goodness helping me do good works?

_____

_____

_____

Hardening my heart towards God's goodness means I am storing up
a treasure of wrath in the day of the righteous judgment of God
(verse 5).

God will render to each one according to his deeds
(Verse 6, Psalm 62:12)

*Indignation, wrath, tribulation, anguish to every soul of man are
stored up by those who are (verses 8-9):*

❑ Self-seeking (verse 8)

❑ Not obeying truth (verse 8)

❑ Obeying unrighteousness (verse 8)

❑ Doing evil (verse 9)

What indicators in my life show that I take these verses seriously?

_____

_____

_____

_____

Day 7: **Romans 2:11-29**

For there is no partiality with God.
> —Romans 2:11 (Deut. 10:17, Psalm 15, Acts 10:34-35, Galatians 2:6)

How does God's equal acceptance of everyone impact my life?

_____

_____

_____

People who do not know God's laws:

- ❏ Naturally do the things in the law (verse 14)

- ❏ Are helped by their conscience to know right from wrong (verse 15)

...[T]he doers of the law will be justified.
> —Romans 2:11

Paul tells us that true doers of the law are only those who inwardly have the laws written on their hearts, follow the Holy Spirit, and receive their praise from God rather from others (verse 29).

How has the Holy Spirit helped me to not just be a hearer of the law, but also a doer?

_____

_____

How does being empowered by the Holy Spirit keep me walking in freedom rather than thinking I can be justified by following the law, rules, and regulations?

_____

_____

_____

Day 8: **Romans 3**

Although the Jews were the first people to receive God's laws:

- ❏ All people are under sin and fall short of the glory of God (verses 9, 23)

- ❏ No flesh will be justified in the sight of God (verse 20)

- ❏ The righteousness of God is through faith and belief in Jesus Christ (verse 22)

- ❏ We are justified freely because of the grace that extends through the redemption in Christ Jesus (verse 24)

- ❏ Christ's blood covers our sins (verse 25)

- ❏ Jesus justifies those who have faith in Him (verse 26)

This passage is the gospel and good news of Jesus for all people.

How can I apply this list to share the gospel so others will be drawn to freedom in Jesus and freedom from sin?

_____

_____

_____

_____

Since no flesh can be justified in the sight of God, what do I do when I wrestle with fleshly desires arising within myself?

_____

_____

_____

_____

_____

Day 9: Romans 4:1-23

This chapter emphasizes that God made it clear through Abraham that people cannot come to Him through works. They need faith and belief. Works of the flesh do not count towards the grace of God. Faith, hope, and belief count as righteousness (verses 1-18).

In old age Abraham had no children, yet God declared:

...I have made you a father of many nations....
—Romans 4:17 (Genesis 17:5)

Abraham's response was this:

He did not waiver at the promise of God through unbelief, but was strengthened in faith, giving glory to God, and being fully convinced that what He had promised He was also able to perform.
—Romans 4:20-21

God was working out His plan for me even during the time of Abraham (verse 23).

What times in my life did my faith in God eventually bear fruit of His promises for me, even when there was no evidence that things would work out at the time?

_____

_____

_____

_____

_____

_____

_____

_____

_____

Day 10: **Romans 4:17-25**

...God, who gives life to the dead and calls those things which do not exist as though they did.

—Romans 4:17

In what seemingly dead or impossible area of my life do I believe God has called me to trust Him? How will I pray according to this verse?

_____

_____

_____

_____

_____

_____

...[I]t shall be imputed to us who believe in Him who raised up Jesus our Lord from the dead, who was delivered up our offenses, and was raised because of our justification.

—Romans 4:24-25 (Isaiah 53:4-6)

When Jesus rose from the dead, He delivered up my offenses and justified me in the presence of God. How has this gift from God changed the way I live?

_____

_____

_____

_____

_____

_____

Day 11: Romans 5:1-5

Because I have been justified by faith in Jesus:

- ❑ I have peace with God (verse 1)

- ❑ I have access to stand in grace (verse 2)

- ❑ I rejoice in hope of the glory of God (verse 2)

How are peace, grace, and hope active in me?

_____

_____

_____

_____

I glory in tribulations, knowing that:

- ❑ Tribulation produces perseverance (verse 3)

- ❑ Perseverance produces character (verse 4)

- ❑ Character produces hope (verse 4)

Now hope does not disappoint, because the love of God has been poured out in our hearts by the Holy Spirit who was given to us.
—Romans 5:5

How does the love of God poured out in my heart help me face tribulations?

_____

_____

_____

_____

_____

Day 12: **Romans 5:6-11**

...[W]e have now received the reconciliation.

—Romans 5:11

- ❑ Christ died for us when we were still without strength (verse 6)

- ❑ While we were still sinners, God demonstrated His own love for us (verse 8)

- ❑ We have been justified from our sins by Christ's blood (verse 9)

- ❑ Through Jesus we are saved from wrath (verse 9)

- ❑ Through Jesus we have received a way to God (verse 11)

How have I received strength, God's love, and a sense of being justified because my sins are forgiven?

_____

_____

_____

_____

_____

_____

_____

_____

_____

_____

_____

_____

_____

Day 13: **Romans 5:12-21**

Sin entered the world through Adam (verse 14, Genesis 2:17, 3:6-9)

The gift of grace, righteousness, and eternal life came through Jesus (verses 15, 17, 21)

But the free gift is not like the offense. For if by the one man's offense many died, much more the grace of God and the gift by the grace of the one Man, Jesus Christ, abounded to many.

—Romans 5:15

Therefore, as through one man's offense judgment came to all men, resulting in condemnation, even so through one Man's righteous act the free gift came to all men, resulting in justification of life.

—Romans 5:18

For as by one man's disobedience many were made sinners, so also by one Man's obedience many will be made righteous.

—Romans 5:19

To what extent do I rejoice that I live with the ability to be reconciled to God and not live under judgment?

_____

_____

_____

How can I express gratitude to the Lord throughout my day?

_____

_____

_____

_____

_____

Day 14: **Romans 6:1-14**

...[W]e also should walk in newness of life.

—Romans 6:4

This list is a reminder of all the ways that baptism into Jesus has transformed my life:

- ❑ He died on the cross; I also died and was buried with Him (verse 4)

- ❑ He was raised from the dead; I also was raised with Him and given an opportunity to walk in new life (verse 4)

- ❑ My old self was crucified with Him (verse 6)

- ❑ I am no longer a slave to sin (verse 6)

- ❑ I am dead to sin and freed from sin (verses 7, 11)

Which of these is the most meaningful to me right now? Why?

_____

_____

Therefore do not let sin reign in your mortal body, that you should obey it in its lusts.

—Romans 6:12 (Genesis 4:7)

...[P]resent yourselves to God as being alive from the dead, and your members [bodies] as instruments of righteousness to God. For sin shall not have dominion over you....

—Romans 6:13-14

How do I present my body to God so sin has no dominion over me?

_____

_____

_____

_____

Day 15: **Romans 6:15-23**

Do you not know that to whom you present yourselves slaves to obey, you are that one's slaves whom you obey, whether of sin leading to death, or of obedience leading to righteousness?
—Romans 6:16

I am a slave to sin or to righteousness, one or the other. Which have I chosen and how does that make a difference in my life?

_____

_____

But God be thanked that though you were slaves of sin...having been set free from sin, you became slaves of righteousness... for holiness.
—Romans 6:17-19

How has being a slave to righteousness given me strength and desire for more and more holiness (sanctification) in my life?

_____

_____

But now having been set free from sin, and having become slaves of God, you have your fruit to holiness, and the end everlasting life.
—Romans 6:22

What is the Lord doing in me to produce fruit that is holy?

_____

_____

Since presenting myself to God in obedience leads to eternal life, how does this impact me in everything I think or do?

_____

_____

Day 16: **Romans 7:1-6**

Paul begins Chapter 7 by saying he is speaking to those who know the law, referring to the 10 Commandments and the Old Testament laws given by God (verse 1).

...[T]he law has dominion over a man as long as he lives.
—Romans 7:1

Since we have died to the law through the body of Christ's death, we are now raised from the dead, that we should bear fruit to God (verse 4).

For when we were in the flesh, the sinful passions which were aroused by the law were at work in our members [bodies] to bear fruit to death. But now we have been delivered from the law, having died to what we were held by, so that we should serve in the newness of the Spirit and not in the oldness of the letter [law].
—Romans 7:5-6

Why might God allow me to choose to follow His laws rather than force me to follow them?

_____

_____

_____

_____

How does serving with the Spirit's leading impact my sense of freedom?

_____

_____

_____

_____

_____

_____

Day 17: **Romans 7:7-25**

The laws and commandments of God are holy, just, good, and spiritual. Because I am carnal, they expose my sin, which is unholy, unjust, and evil (verse 12-14).

For I know that in me (that is, in my flesh) nothing good dwells; for to will is present with me, but *how* to perform what is good I do not find.

—Romans 7:18

For the good that I will to do, I do not do; but the evil I will not to do, that I practice.

—Romans 7:19

Do I currently have a struggle with my flesh that keeps me in a pattern of practicing or dwelling on evil? Explain.

_____

_____

_____

_____

_____

O wretched man that I am! Who will deliver me from this body of death? I thank God—through Jesus Christ our Lord...!

—Romans 7:24-25

How have I experienced Jesus helping me overcome a pattern of sin?

_____

_____

_____

_____

_____

Day 18: **Romans 8:1-13**

There is therefore now no condemnation to those who are in Christ Jesus, who do not walk according to the flesh, but according to the Spirit.

—Romans 8:1

I am not condemned if these are active in my life:

❑ I am in Christ Jesus (verse 1)

❑ I walk not according to my fleshly desires (verse 1)

❑ I walk according to the Holy Spirit living in me (verse 1)

Is there any area of my life in which I deal with condemnation? How can I apply these truths?

_____

_____

_____

These are true about walking in the flesh:

❑ If I live according to the flesh, my mind is *set* on the things of the flesh (verse 5)

❑ Having a carnal mind is death (verse 6, 13)

❑ A carnal mind is enmity against God (verse 7)

❑ If I am in the flesh, I cannot please God (verse 8)

❑ If I walk in the flesh, I do not have the Spirit of Christ and do not belong to Him (verse 9)

Describe what walking in the flesh looked/looks like in my life?

_____

_____

_____

Day 19: **Romans 8:1-16**

When walking in the Holy Spirit:

❏ There is no condemnation (verse 1)

❏ I am free from the law of sin and death (verse 2)

❏ The righteous requirement of the law is fulfilled in me (verse 4)

❏ My mind is set on the things of the Spirit (verse 5)

❏ I have life and peace (verse 6, 11,13)

❏ I please God (verse 8)

❏ I belong to Christ (verse 9, 14)

❏ I can call God, Daddy; I am a child of God (verse 15, 16)

Which of these attributes of walking in the Spirit are active in me?

_____

_____

_____

_____

_____

How is my mind set on the things of the Spirit?

_____

_____

_____

_____

_____

_____

Day 20: **Romans 8:17-25**

...[W]e are children of God, and if children, then heirs—heirs of God and joint heirs with Christ, if indeed we suffer with Him, that we may also be glorified together.

—Romans 8:16-17

What does suffering with Christ mean in my life?

_____

_____

_____

For I consider that the sufferings of this present time are not worthy to be compared with the glory which shall be revealed in us.

—Romans 8:18

What glory of Christ has been revealed in me?

_____

_____

_____

[We] ourselves groan within ourselves, eagerly waiting for the adoption, the redemption of our body. But if we hope for what we do not see, we eagerly wait for it with perseverance.

—Romans 8:23, 25

How does hope help me persevere?

_____

_____

_____

_____

_____

Day 21: **Romans 8:26-28**

...[T]he Spirit helps us in our weaknesses. For we do not know what we should pray for... but the Spirit Himself makes intercession for us... according to the will of God.

—Romans 8:26, 27

How does it help me to realize that the Holy Spirit is interceding in my weaknesses according to the will of God?

_____

_____

_____

_____

And we know that all things work together for good to those who love God, to those who are the called according to His purpose.

—Romans 8:28

How confident am I that God is working all things for my good?

< 1 – 2 – 3 – 4 – 5 – 6 – 7 – 8 – 9 – 10 > (circle one and explain)

_____

_____

_____

_____

How does my life align with the calling I have to live by His purpose?

_____

_____

_____

_____

_____

Day 22: **Romans 8:29-39**

God has:

- ☐ Called me (verse 30)

- ☐ Justified me (verse 30)

- ☐ Glorified me (verse 30)

...If God is for us, who can be against us? Who shall bring a charge against God's elect? It is God who justifies.

—Romans 8:31, 33

Am I fearful of anyone or anything?

_____

_____

_____

How do I explain that God has called, justified, and glorified me?

_____

_____

_____

This is my confidence:

- ☐ Christ has died and risen from the dead (verse 34)

- ☐ Christ is at the right hand of God (verse 34)

- ☐ Christ makes intercession for me (verse 34)

Christ will not allow anything to separate me from His love (verse 35-39).

Yet in all these things we are more than conquerors through Him who loved us.

—Romans 8:37

Day 23: **Romans 9:1-18**

I tell you the truth in Christ, I am not lying, my conscience also bearing me witness in the Holy Spirit….

—Romans 9:1

My belief in what Paul says impacts how I view scripture. Do I believe what he says, or am I skeptical and dismiss some of what he says? Do I hold scripture at arm's length or do I receive it as truth?

_____

_____

_____

Paul is grieved and willing to do anything for his Israelite relatives, if only they would believe in God's promises through Jesus (verses 2-14).

Paul understood the Jewish struggle to come to terms with God's purposes in light of His mercy, grace, and will.

For He says to Moses, "I will have mercy on whomever I will have mercy, and I will have compassion on whomever I will have compassion." So then it is not of him who wills, nor of him who runs, but of God who shows mercy.

—Romans 9:15-16 (Exodus 33:19)

For the scripture says to the Pharaoh, "For this very purpose I have raised you up, that I may show My power in you, and that My name may be declared in all the earth." Therefore He has mercy on whom He wills, and whom He wills He hardens.

—Romans 9:17-18 (Exodus 9:16)

What do I do when I encounter scripture that does not fit easily into my mindset, preferences, or willingness to trust God?

_____

_____

_____

Day 24: **Romans 9:19-33**

...[W]ho are you to reply against God? Will the thing formed say to Him who formed it, "Why have you made me like this?"
—Romans 9:20 (Isaiah 29:16)

Does not the potter have power over the clay, from the same lump to make one vessel for honor and another for dishonor?
—Romans 9:21

How much do I question how God has made me?

_____

_____

_____

_____

_____

Paul explains that the Israelites could not receive the law of righteousness because they did not seek it by faith. But God provided a way through Jesus for people to attain righteousness (verse 22-31, Hosea 1:10, 2:23, Isaiah 1:9, 10:22,23).

...[W]hoever believes on Him will not be put to shame.
—Romans 9:33 (Romans 10:11, Isaiah 8:14, 28:16)

How does seeking Jesus take away all my shame?

_____

_____

_____

_____

_____

_____

_____

Day 25: **Romans 10:1-9**

Paul expresses once again his yearning for the people of Israel to be saved by believing and receiving Jesus (verse 1).

He described their spiritual condition this way:

❑ They have a zeal for God, but not according to knowledge (verse 2)

❑ They are ignorant of God's righteousness (verse 3)

❑ They seek to establish their own righteousness (verse 3)

❑ They have not submitted to the righteousness of God (verse 3)

How am I increasing my zeal for God, knowledge of God, and submission to God?

_____

_____

_____

But the righteousness of faith speaks this way (verse 6):

❑ The Word is near you (verse 8, Deut. 30:14)

❑ The Word is in your mouth (verse 8, Deut. 30:14)

❑ The Word is in your heart (verse 8, Deut. 30:14)

...[I]f you confess with your mouth the Lord Jesus and believe in your heart that God has raised Him from the dead, you will be saved.
—Romans 10:9

When and how did this happen for me?

_____

_____

_____

Day 26: Romans 10:1-21

...[T]he same Lord over all is rich to all who call upon Him.
—Romans 10:12

For "whoever calls on the name of the Lord shall be saved."
—Romans 10:13 (Joel 2:32)

How and when has the Lord's richness reached to me and those close to me?

_____

_____

_____

How beautiful are the feet of those who preach the gospel of peace, who bring glad tidings of good things!
—Romans 10:15 (Isaiah 52:7, Nahum 1:15)

- ❑ How then shall they call on Him in whom they have not believed? (verse 14)

- ❑ And how shall they believe in Him of whom they have not heard? (verse 14)

- ❑ And how shall they hear without a preacher? (verse 14)

- ❑ And how shall they preach unless they are sent? (verse 15)

...[F]aith comes by hearing, and hearing by the word of God.
—Romans 10:17

What are my favorite examples of seeing people being drawn to the gospel?

_____

_____

_____

_____

Day 27: **Romans 11:1-27**

Paul shares concern for his Jewish relatives as he ministers to the Gentiles.

Therefore consider the goodness and severity of God: on those who fell, severity; but toward you, goodness, if you continue in His goodness. Otherwise you also will be cut off.

—Romans 11:22

How do I see God?

- ❑ As all goodness

- ❑ As all severity

- ❑ As a mix of both goodness and severity

How do I gain comfort from His goodness?

_____

_____

What are my emotions concerning the severity of God?

_____

_____

_____

…[A]ll Israel will be saved, as it is written: "The Deliverer will come out of Zion, and He will turn away ungodliness from Jacob; for this is My covenant with them, when I take away their sins."

—Romans 11:26, 27 (Isaiah 59:20)

How am I resting in the covenant of my sins being taken away?

_____

_____

_____

Day 28: Romans 11:28-36

For the gifts and the calling of God are irrevocable.
—Romans 11:29 (Numbers 23:19)

Which gifts and calling of God are irrevocable in my life?

_____

_____

_____

_____

Oh, the depth of the riches both of the wisdom and knowledge of God! How unsearchable are His judgments and His ways past finding out!
—Romans 11:33

❑ Can I know the mind of the Lord? (verse 34, Isaiah 40:13, Jeremiah 25:18)

❑ Can I become His counselor? (verse 34, Jeremiah 23:18)

❑ Does the Lord owe me? (verse 34, Job 41:11)

For of Him and through Him and to Him are all things, to whom be glory forever. Amen.
—Romans 11:36

How do I seek the deep things of God that seem mysterious?

_____

_____

_____

_____

_____

_____

Day 29: **Romans 12:1-2**

[B]y the mercies of God, that you present your bodies....

—Romans 12:1

❑ A living sacrifice (verse 1)

❑ Holy (verse 1)

❑ Acceptable to God (verse 1)

In what condition is my body, inside and out, as I present it to God?

_____

_____

_____

_____

And do not be conformed to this world, but be transformed by the renewing of your mind, that you may prove what is that good and acceptable and perfect will of God.

—Romans 12:2

Which parts of my mind and thoughts still need transformation?

_____

_____

_____

_____

How easy or difficult is it to keep my mind focused on His will?

_____

_____

_____

_____

Day 30: **Romans 12:3-8**

Transformation impacts how I function in the body of Christ.

For I [Paul] say, through the grace given to me, to everyone who is among you, not to think of himself more highly than he ought to think, but to think soberly, as God has dealt to each one a measure of faith.

—Romans 12:3

How accurately do I live up to the measure of faith God gave me?

_____

_____

_____

...[W]e are one body in Christ, and individually members of one another. Having then gifts differing according to the grace that is given to us, let us use them....

—Romans 12:5-6

❑ Gifts of Prophecy use in proportion to our faith (verse 6)

❑ Gifts of Ministry use in proportion to our faith (verse 7)

❑ Gifts of Teaching use in proportion to our faith (verse 7)

❑ Gifts of Exhorting use in proportion to our faith (verse 8)

❑ Gifts of Giving, with liberality (verse 8)

❑ Gifts of Leading, with diligence (verse 8)

❑ Gifts of Mercy, with cheerfulness (verse 8)

Which of these gifts has God graced to me? How am I using them?

_____

_____

_____

_____

Day 31: **Romans 12:9-11**

How I am doing in each of these areas?

❑ Loving without hypocrisy (verse 9)

< 1 – 2 – 3 – 4 – 5 – 6 – 7 – 8 – 9 – 10 > (circle one and explain)

_____

❑ Abhorring what is evil (verse 9)

< 1 – 2 – 3 – 4 – 5 – 6 – 7 – 8 – 9 – 10 > (circle one and explain)

_____

❑ Clinging to what is good (verse 9)

< 1 – 2 – 3 – 4 – 5 – 6 – 7 – 8 – 9 – 10 > (circle one and explain)

_____

❑ Showing kindness and affection with brotherly love (verse 10)

< 1 – 2 – 3 – 4 – 5 – 6 – 7 – 8 – 9 – 10 > (circle one and explain)

_____

❑ Honoring and giving preference to others (verse 10)

< 1 – 2 – 3 – 4 – 5 – 6 – 7 – 8 – 9 – 10 > (circle one and explain)

_____

_____

❑ Not lagging in diligence (verse 11)

< 1 – 2 – 3 – 4 – 5 – 6 – 7 – 8 – 9 – 10 > (circle one and explain)

_____

_____

_____

Day 32: Romans 12:11-13

How I am doing in each of these areas?

☐ Fervent (passionate intensity) in spirit (verse 11)

< 1 – 2 – 3 – 4 – 5 – 6 – 7 – 8 – 9 – 10 > (circle one and explain)

_____

☐ Serving the Lord (verse 11)

< 1 – 2 – 3 – 4 – 5 – 6 – 7 – 8 – 9 – 10 > (circle one and explain)

_____

☐ Rejoicing in hope (verse 12)

< 1 – 2 – 3 – 4 – 5 – 6 – 7 – 8 – 9 – 10 > (circle one and explain)

_____

☐ Patient in tribulation (verse 12)

< 1 – 2 – 3 – 4 – 5 – 6 – 7 – 8 – 9 – 10 > (circle one and explain)

_____

☐ Continuing steadfastly in prayer (verse 12)

< 1 – 2 – 3 – 4 – 5 – 6 – 7 – 8 – 9 – 10 > (circle one and explain)

_____

_____

☐ Distributing to the needs of the saints (verse 13)

< 1 – 2 – 3 – 4 – 5 – 6 – 7 – 8 – 9 – 10 > (circle one and explain)

_____

_____

_____

Day 33: **Romans 12:13-16**

How I am doing in each of these areas?

❑ Given to hospitality (verse 13)

< 1 – 2 – 3 – 4 – 5 – 6 – 7 – 8 – 9 – 10 > (circle one and explain)

_____

❑ Blessing and not cursing those who persecute me (verse 14)

< 1 – 2 – 3 – 4 – 5 – 6 – 7 – 8 – 9 – 10 > (circle one and explain)

_____

❑ Rejoicing with those who rejoice (verse 15)

< 1 – 2 – 3 – 4 – 5 – 6 – 7 – 8 – 9 – 10 > (circle one and explain)

_____

❑ Weeping with those who weep (verse 15)

< 1 – 2 – 3 – 4 – 5 – 6 – 7 – 8 – 9 – 10 > (circle one and explain)

_____

❑ Not setting my mind on high things, but associating with the humble (verse 16)

< 1 – 2 – 3 – 4 – 5 – 6 – 7 – 8 – 9 – 10 > (circle one and explain)

_____

_____

❑ Not being wise in my own opinion (verse 16)

< 1 – 2 – 3 – 4 – 5 – 6 – 7 – 8 – 9 – 10 > (circle one and explain)

_____

_____

_____

Day 34: **Romans 12:17-21**

How I am doing in each of these areas?

❑ Repaying no one evil for evil (verse 17)

< 1 – 2 – 3 – 4 – 5 – 6 – 7 – 8 – 9 – 10 > (circle one and explain)

_____

❑ Having regard for good things in the sight of all people (verse 17)

< 1 – 2 – 3 – 4 – 5 – 6 – 7 – 8 – 9 – 10 > (circle one and explain)

_____

If it is possible, as much as depends on you, live peaceably with all men.
                                                        —Romans 12:18

How easy or difficult is this for me to live out?

_____

_____

_____

_____

"Vengeance is Mine, I will repay," says the Lord.
                                    —Romans 12:19 (Deuteronomy 32:35)

Do not be overcome by evil, but overcome evil with good.
                                                        —Romans 12:21

What good things can I do to help overcome evil?

_____

_____

_____

_____

Day 35: **Romans 13**

Let every soul be subject to the governing authorities. For there is no authority except from God, and the authorities that exist are appointed by God. Therefore whoever resists the authority resists the ordinance of God, and those who resist will bring judgment on themselves.

—Romans 13:1-2

Do I tend to embrace or resist authority with which I disagree?

_____

_____

Owe no one anything except to love one another….

—Romans 13:8

Love does no harm…

—Romans 13:10

How can loving like this be easy or difficult for me?

_____

_____

…[C]ast off the works of darkness, and let us put on the armor of light. But put on the Lord Jesus Christ, and make no provision for the flesh, to fulfill its lusts.

—Romans 13:12, 14

Are there any works of darkness that I need to cast off?

_____

_____

How does putting on the armor of light and the Lord Jesus help me keep from making provision for my flesh?

_____

_____

Day 36: **Romans 14:1-13**

For none of us lives to himself, and no one dies to himself. For if we live, we live to the Lord; and if we die, we die to the Lord.
—Romans 14:7-8

❏ But why do you judge your brother? (verse 10)

❏ Or why do you show contempt for your brother? (verse 10)

…For we shall all stand before the judgment seat of Christ. So then each of us shall give account of himself to God.
—Romans 14:10,12

When am I most easily tempted to judge or show contempt for others?

_____

_____

_____

What does that answer reveal about my character?

_____

_____

_____

Therefore let us not judge one another anymore, but rather resolve this, not to put a stumbling block or a cause to fall in our brother's way.
—Romans 14:13

Do I error on the side of caring or not caring if I offend someone or cause them to stumble?

_____

_____

_____

_____

Day 37: **Romans 14:14-23**

The kingdom of God is:

❑ Righteousness in the Holy Spirit (verse 17)

❑ Peace in the Holy Spirit (verse 17)

❑ Joy in the Holy Spirit (verse 17)

In which of these do I most experience the Holy Spirit?

_____

_____

_____

How do I see these things in myself impacting the kingdom of God?

_____

_____

_____

...[P]ursue the things which make for peace and the things by which one may edify another.

—Romans 14:19

What things do I pursue that make for peace?

_____

_____

_____

What things am I pursuing which may edify others?

_____

_____

_____

Day 38: **Romans 15:1-14**

Let each of us please his neighbor for his good, leading to edification... [T]hat you may with one mind and one mouth glorify the God and Father of our Lord Jesus Christ.

—Romans 15:2, 6

How willing am I pleasing my neighbor until they are built up, encouraged, and we have unity?

< 1 – 2 – 3 – 4 – 5 – 6 – 7 – 8 – 9 – 10 > (circle one and explain)

_____

_____

_____

...[T]hat we through the patience and comfort of the Scriptures might have hope.

—Romans 15:4

How have the Scriptures given me hope?

_____

_____

_____

Now may the God of hope fill you with all joy and peace in believing, that you may abound in hope by the power of the Holy Spirit.

—Romans 15:13

How can I grow to abound in more hope, joy, and peace?

_____

_____

_____

_____

Day 39: Romans 15:15-16:16

Therefore I have reason to glory in Christ Jesus in the things which pertain to God. For I will not dare to speak of any of those things which Christ has not accomplished through me, in word and deed....

—Romans 15:17, 18

How does Paul's life of ministry invigorate me or intimidate me?

_____

_____

_____

In Romans 16 Paul affectionately greets the believers in Rome. Here are some of the attributes of the people he mentions:

❑ A servant of the church (verse 16:1)

❑ A helper of many (verse 16:2)

❑ Fellow workers and laborers in the Lord (verse 16:3,9,12)

❑ They risk their own necks for those in the body of Christ (verse 16:4)

❑ My countrymen, family, and fellow prisoners in the Lord (verse 16:7,13)

❑ Approved in Christ, chosen in the Lord (verse 16:10,13)

How have these attributes affected my own fellowship experience in the body of Christ?

_____

_____

_____

Greet one another with a holy kiss.

—Romans 16:16

Day 40: **Romans 16:17-27**

Paul concludes the book of Romans with two warnings and an encouragement for God's people.

Now I urge you, brethren, note those who cause divisions and offenses, contrary to the doctrine which you learned, and avoid them.

—Romans 16:17

How do I apply this in my life?

_____

_____

For those who are such do not serve our Lord Jesus Christ, but their own belly, and by smooth words and flattering speech deceive the hearts of the simple.

—Romans 16:18

How do I discern smooth, flattering, and deceptive words?

_____

_____

_____

...[B]ut I want you to be wise in what is good, and simple concerning evil. And the God of peace will crush Satan under your feet shortly... [T]o God, alone wise, be glory through Jesus Christ forever. Amen.

—Romans 16:19, 20, 27

What does it mean to me to be wise in what is good and simple in what is evil?

_____

_____

_____

NEW TESTAMENT

42 Days

In

I CORINTHIANS

Day 1: **1 Corinthians 1:1-8**

Paul, called to be an apostle of Jesus Christ through the will of God...

—1 Corinthians 1:1

Paul is writing to:

- ❑ The church of God at Corinth (verse 2)

- ❑ To those who are sanctified in Christ Jesus (verse 2)

- ❑ To those who are called to be saints (verse 2)

- ❑ To those *in* every place who call on the name of Jesus Christ our Lord (verse 2)

Paul's focus:

- ❑ I thank God always concerning you for the grace of God which was given to you by Christ Jesus (verse 4)

- ❑ That you are enriched in everything in all that you say and all knowledge (verse 5)

- ❑ The testimony of Christ is confirmed *in you* (verse 6)

- ❑ That you come up short in no gift, eagerly waiting for the revelation of our Lord Jesus Christ (verse 7)

- ❑ That you may be blameless to the end (verse 8)

How can I turn these into a prayer for others and myself today?

_____

_____

_____

_____

_____

_____

Day 2: **1 Corinthians 1:9-13**

God is faithful, by whom you were called into the fellowship of His Son, Jesus Christ our Lord.

—1 Corinthians 1:9

Believers in Jesus are called to fellowship with other believers.

Paul pleads with the brothers and sisters in Christ:

- ❑ To all speak the same thing concerning our faith and beliefs according to what they had been taught concerning the message of the cross (verse 10,13)

- ❑ To be perfectly joined together in the same mind (verse 10)

- ❑ To be perfectly joined together in the same judgment (verse 10)

How would I describe my fellowship experience with Jesus?

_____

_____

_____

_____

_____

How would I describe my fellowship experience with other believers?

_____

_____

_____

_____

_____

_____

Day 3: **1 Corinthians 1:14-20**

For Christ did not send me to baptize, but to preach the gospel, not with wisdom of words, lest the cross of Christ should be made of no effect. For the message of the cross is foolishness to those who are perishing, but to us who are being saved it is the power of God.
—1 Corinthians 1:17-18

How has the power of God and the cross of Christ affected me?

_____

_____

_____

_____

For it is written: "I will destroy the wisdom of the wise, and bring to nothing the understanding of the prudent."
—1 Corinthians 1:19 (Isaiah 29:14)

- ❑ Where are the wise? (verse 20)

- ❑ Where are the scribes? (verse 20)

- ❑ Where are the disputers of this age? (verse 20)

- ❑ Has not God made foolish the wisdom of this world? (verse 20)

How is my walk with the Lord impacted by the wisdom of the world?

_____

_____

_____

_____

_____

_____

Day 4: **1 Corinthians 1:15-31**

...[T]o those who are called...Christ the power of God and the wisdom of God.
—1 Corinthians 1:24

How is Christ's power working in me?

_____

_____

How is Christ's wisdom working in me?

_____

_____

But God has chosen the foolish things of the world to put to shame the wise, and God has chosen the weak things of the world to put to shame the things which are mighty... that no flesh should glory in His presence.
—1 Corinthians 1:27, 29

In my life, what does it mean to be foolish or weak, and to put to shame things that are mighty?

_____

_____

_____

...[H]e who glories, let him glory in the Lord.
—1 Corinthians 1:31 (Jeremiah 9:24)

What is one way I can glory in the Lord today?

_____

_____

_____

_____

Day 5: **1 Corinthians 2:1-5**

...[Y]our faith should not be in the wisdom of men but in the power of God.

—1 Corinthians 2:5

Paul describes his condition when coming to the Corinthians:

- ❑ I did not come with excellent speech (verse 1)

- ❑ I did not come with wisdom declaring the testimony of God (verse 1)

- ❑ The only thing I claim to know is Jesus Christ crucified (verse 2)

- ❑ I came in weakness (verse 3)

- ❑ I came in fear (verse 3)

- ❑ I came trembling (verse 3)

- ❑ My preaching was not with persuasive words of human wisdom (verse 4)

- ❑ My words were in the demonstration of the Spirit (verse 4)

- ❑ My words were in the demonstration of the power of God (verse 5)

How does this example of sharing the gospel of Christ translate into how I might share the gospel with others?

_____

_____

_____

_____

_____

_____

_____

Day 6: 1 Corinthians 2:6-16

But it is written: "Eye has not seen, nor ear heard, nor have entered into the heart of man the things which God has prepared for those who love Him."

—1 Corinthians 2:9 (Isaiah 64:4, 65:17)

But God has revealed them to us through His Spirit....

—1 Corinthians 2:10

This is what I received through the Holy Spirit by believing in Jesus:

- ❑ I know the things of God (verse 11)

- ❑ I know the things that have been freely given to me by God (verse 12)

- ❑ I am taught by the Holy Spirit how to discern spiritual things (verse 13)

- ❑ I do not consider the things of God foolish (verse 14)

- ❑ I judge (discern) all things because I am spiritual (verse 15)

- ❑ I am judged by no one (verse 15)

- ❑ I have the mind of Christ (verse 16)

How am I doing with each of these?

_____

_____

_____

_____

_____

_____

_____

_____

Day 7: **1 Corinthians 3:1-17**

Paul refers to Christians who walk more in the flesh than the Spirit as:

- ❑ Babes in Christ (verse 1)

- ❑ Unable to receive the deep things of God (verse 2)

- ❑ They deal with envy, strife, and divisions with other brothers and sisters in Christ (verse 3)

- ❑ They are divided about to whom they should listen (verse 4-5)

How do I keep myself from walking in these ways?

_____

_____

_____

For no other foundation can anyone lay than that which is laid, which is Jesus Christ.
—1 Corinthians 3:11

When Christ returns, everyone's work built on this foundation will be tested by fire, rewarded or burned (verse 12-14).

Do you not know that you are the temple of God and that the Spirit of God dwells in you? If anyone defiles the temple of God, God will destroy him. For the temple of God is holy, which temple you are.
—1 Corinthians 3:16-17

Since I am housing the Spirit of God, how does this impact the way I treat my body?

_____

_____

_____

_____

Day 8: **1 Corinthians 3:17-23**

Let no one deceive himself. If anyone among you seems to be wise in this age, let him become a fool that he may become wise. For the wisdom of this world is foolishness with God....
—1 Corinthians 3:18-19

How do I view the wisdom of this world?

_____

_____

_____

God's view of the wisdom of the world:

- ❑ The Lord catches them when they think they are crafty (verse 19, Job 5:13)

- ❑ The Lord knows their thoughts are futile (verse 20, Psalm 94:11)

Therefore let no one boast in men. For all things are yours... And you are Christ's, and Christ is God's.
—1 Corinthians 3:21, 23

Do I rely more on people than on God, or do I rely more on God than on people?

_____

_____

_____

What does having all things through Christ look like in my life?

_____

_____

_____

Day 9: **1 Corinthians 4:1-5**

Paul describes how he views being judged:

- ❑ He considers it a small thing to be judged by others (verse 3)

- ❑ He considers it a small thing to be judged by a human court (verse 3)

- ❑ He does not judge or justify himself (verse 3-4)

- ❑ He leaves the judging up to the Lord (verse 4)

How does my view of judgment line up with Paul's view?

_____

_____

_____

_____

Therefore judge nothing before the time, until the Lord comes, who will both bring to light the hidden things of darkness and reveal the counsels of the hearts. Then each one's praise will come from God.

—1 Corinthians 4:5

How do I presently allow the light of God's love to reveal the hidden things of darkness and the motives in my heart?

_____

_____

_____

_____

_____

_____

Day 10: **1 Corinthians 4:6-21**

Apostle Paul and those with which he ministered were examples of laying down their lives for the sake of brothers and sisters in Christ. Here are some things they faced:

- ❑ We were condemned to death (verse 9)

- ❑ We have been made spectacles to the world (verse 9)

- ❑ We are fools for Christ's sake (verse 10)

- ❑ We were hungry, thirsty, poorly clothed, beaten, and homeless (verse 11)

- ❑ We were defamed, made as if we were the filth of the world (verse 13)

What have I suffered for the sake of Jesus or my brothers and sisters in Christ?

_____

_____

To what extent would I be willing to suffer for Jesus and my brothers and sisters in Christ?

_____

_____

For the kingdom of God is not in word but in power.
—1 Corinthians 4:20

How am I going to walk in that power today?

_____

_____

_____

_____

Day 11: **1 Corinthians 5:1-5**

It is actually reported that there is sexual immorality among you....
—1 Corinthians 5:1

Here was what was going on:

- ❏ There was sexual immorality among those who were Christians (verse 1, 4)

- ❏ They were involved with sexual perversion that even non-Christians would not approve (verse 1)

- ❏ They were arrogant about it and unrepentant (verse 2)

How have I been impacted with this in the body of Christ (without naming people)?

_____

_____

_____

This was Paul's recommendation about how to deal with sexual immorality among believers:

- ❏ When you gather together to confront this person come together in the name and power of the Lord Jesus Christ (verse 4)

- ❏ Deliver the person over to Satan so the flesh can be destroyed, and his/her spirit saved in the Day of the Lord Jesus' return (verse 5)

How seriously do I take sexual immorality among believers?

_____

_____

_____

Day 12: **1 Corinthians 5:6-8**

Paul continues to write to believers concerning the needs of the body of Christ in order to persevere in the power of Jesus Christ.

...[D]o you not know that a little leaven leavens the whole lump? Therefore purge out the old leaven, that you may be a new lump, since you truly are unleavened. For indeed Christ, our Passover, was sacrificed for us.

—1 Corinthians 5:6-7 (Isaiah 53:7-10)

Therefore let us keep the feast, not with old leaven, nor with the leaven of malice and wickedness, but with the unleavened bread of sincerity and truth.

—1 Corinthians 5:8

What does it look like in my life to keep out the old leaven and keep the new bread of sincerity and truth?

_____

_____

_____

_____

What impact does it have on me when those in the body of believers are sincere and truthful versus malicious and wicked?

_____

_____

_____

_____

_____

_____

_____

Day 13: 1 Corinthians 5:9-11

Paul continues to explain what it means to deal with sin in the body of believers.

I wrote to you in my epistle not to keep company with sexually immoral people. Yet I certainly did not mean with the sexually immoral people of this world, or with the covetous, or extortioners, or idolaters, since then you would need to go out of the world. But now I have written to you not to keep company with anyone named a brother….

—1 Corinthians 5:9-11

Here is a list of those not to keep company with, or even eat with, in the body of Christ (verses 11):

- ❑ The sexually immoral (verse 11)

- ❑ Those who covet (verse 11)

- ❑ Idolaters (verse 11)

- ❑ Revelers (verse 11)

- ❑ Drunkards (verse 11)

- ❑ Extortioners (verse 11)

Am I in close company or friendship with someone who claims to be a believer but engages in these things? If so, what is my response to them?

_____

_____

_____

_____

_____

_____

Day 14: **1 Corinthians 5:9-6:8**

For what do I have to do with judging those also who are outside? Do you not judge those who are inside? But those who are outside God judges. Therefore "put away from yourselves the evil person."
—1 Corinthians 5:12-13 (Deut. 17:2)

How do I come to terms with this verse?

_____

_____

_____

Dare any of you, having a matter against another, go to law before the unrighteous, and not before the saints?
—1 Corinthians 6:1

Do you not know that the saints will judge the world...?
—1 Corinthians 6:2

...[A]nd if the world will be judged by you, are you unworthy to judge the smallest matters?
—1 Corinthians 6:2

Do you not know that we shall judge angels? How much more, things that pertain to this life?
—1 Corinthians 6:3

...[D]o you appoint those who are least esteemed by the church to judge? ...[W]ho will be able to judge between his brethren?
—1 Corinthians 6:4-5

How do I view these passages and apply them to my experience with other believers?

_____

_____

_____

_____

Day 15: **1 Corinthians 6:9-10**

Do you not know that the unrighteous will not inherit the kingdom of God? Do not be deceived….

—1 Corinthians 6:9

These will not inherit the kingdom of God (verse 10):

- ❑ Fornicators (verse 9)

- ❑ Idolaters (verse 9)

- ❑ Adulterers (verse 9)

- ❑ Homosexuals (verse 9)

- ❑ Sodomites (verse 9

- ❑ Thieves (verse 10)

- ❑ Coveters (verse 10)

- ❑ Drunkards (verse 10)

- ❑ Revilers (verse 10)

- ❑ Extortioners (verse 10)

Do I error on the side of believing what the scripture says here, or do I error on the side of unbelief?

_____

_____

_____

In which of the above list are my greatest temptations to engage?

_____

_____

_____

_____

Day 16: **1 Corinthians 6:11-20**

And such were some of you. But you were washed, but you were sanctified, but you were justified in the name of the Lord Jesus and by the Spirit of our God.

—1 Corinthians 6:11

How have Jesus and the Spirit of God washed, sanctified, and justified me?

_____

_____

Or do you not know that your body is the temple of the Holy Spirit who is in you, whom you have from God, and you are not your own? For you were bought at a price; therefore glorify God in your body and in your spirit, which are God's.

—1 Corinthians 6:19-20

Do I view my body more as my own or God's?

_____

_____

_____

How do I glorify God in my body?

_____

_____

_____

How do I glorify God in my spirit?

_____

_____

_____

Day 17: 1 Corinthians 7:1-40

In verse 1-16 Paul distinguishes the commands of the Lord versus his own thoughts concerning husbands and wives. This is what he says about the Lord's command:

Now to the married I command, yet not I but the Lord: a wife is not to depart from her husband. But even if she does depart, let her remain unmarried or be reconciled to her husband. And a husband is not to divorce his wife.

—1 Corinthians 7:10-11

Have I witnessed a Christian remaining unmarried after divorce? Have I witnessed reconciliation between a husband and wife after separation? How am I influenced by this passage?

_____

_____

_____

_____

_____

...[K]eeping the commandments of God is what matters. You were bought at a price; do not become slaves of men.

—1 Corinthians 7:19, 23

How do I serve those I love and those I work for without becoming a slave to them?

_____

_____

_____

_____

_____

Day 18: 1 Corinthians 8:1-13

Now concerning things offered to idols… [A]n idol is nothing in the world, and that there is no other God but one… yet for us there is one God, the Father, of whom are all things, and we for Him; and one Lord Jesus Christ… through whom we live.

—1 Corinthians 8:1, 4, 6

Although I live in Jesus' liberty free from serving idols, I still need to consider that the impact of my words and actions upon my weaker brothers and sisters in Christ could lead them to stumble (verse 1-10).

And because of your knowledge shall the weak brother perish, for whom Christ died? But when you thus sin against the brethren, and wound their weak conscience, you sin against Christ.

—1 Corinthians 8:11-12

How concerned am I that my behavior has impact on my brothers and sisters in Christ?

< 1 – 2 – 3 – 4 – 5 – 6 – 7 – 8 – 9 – 10 > (circle one and explain)

_____

_____

_____

_____

How am I doing when it comes to loving and caring for those in the body of Christ?

_____

_____

_____

_____

_____

Day 19: **1 Corinthians 9:1-27**

In Chapter 9, Paul describes how he has not partaken of some of the benefits that were rightfully his to expect as a minister of the gospel. Here are some of his reasons:

- ❏ He presented the gospel of Christ without charge (even though he had every right to be given provision), so he would not abuse his authority in the gospel (verses 4-18)

- ❏ He made himself a servant to all, so he could win more to Christ (verse 19)

- ❏ He met people wherever they were in life so he could walk with them for the gospel's sake (verse 20-27)

How is my calling different than Paul's calling?

_____

_____

_____

What would need to change in my life in order for me to make the type of sacrifices Paul made for the sake of the gospel?

_____

_____

_____

_____

How am I, or how can I be, a servant to all those around me?

_____

_____

_____

_____

Day 20: **1 Corinthians 10:1-12**

Therefore let him who thinks he stands take heed lest he fall.
—1 Corinthians 10:12

Paul explains how the children of Israel were all God's children walking together, seeing God's mighty power, and drinking from the same spiritual Rock. Even so, many of them were not pleasing God with their behavior. (verses 1-5)

Here are some of the ways they did not please God, as an example to us (verse 6, 11):

- ❑ Do not lust after evil things as they did (verse 6, Numbers 11:4,34)

- ❑ Do not become idolaters like some of them became (verse 7, Exodus 32:6)

- ❑ Do not commit sexual immorality as some of them did (verse 8, Numbers 25:1-13, 31:16)

- ❑ Do not *tempt* Christ as some of them did (verse 9, Exodus 17:2,7)

- ❑ Do not *complain* as they complained (verse 10, Exodus 16,2)

How are these examples helpful to me?

_____

_____

_____

How do these examples draw me near to Jesus or make me run from Him?

_____

_____

_____

_____

Day 21: 1 Corinthians 10:13-22

No temptation has overtaken you except such as is common to man; but God is faithful, who will not allow you to be tempted beyond what you are able, but with the temptation will also make the way of escape, that you may be able to bear it.
—1 Corinthians 10:13

What are some examples from my life when I did not think there was a way out of my temptations?

_____

_____

_____

_____

Do I have examples of times when I had victory over temptation?

_____

_____

_____

_____

...I do not want you to have fellowship with demons. You cannot drink the cup of the Lord and the cup of demons; you cannot partake of the Lord's table and of the table of demons.
—1 Corinthians 10:20-21 (Lev. 17:7, Deut. 32:17)

How do I discern and determine what is of God and what is demonic?

_____

_____

_____

_____

Day 22: **1 Corinthians 10:23-33**

…[N]ot all things edify. Let no one seek his own, but each one the other's well-being…Give no offense… [N]ot seeking my own profit… that they may be saved.

—1 Corinthians 10:23-24, 32-33

How do I ensure that I am contributing to the well-being of others and building them up?

_____

_____

_____

_____

What examples in my life do I have of people being saved because someone put aside their own agenda for the sake of others? How have I done this?

_____

_____

_____

_____

…[W]hatever you do, do all to the glory of God.

—1 Corinthians 10:31

How can I apply this in my life?

_____

_____

_____

_____

_____

Day 23: **1 Corinthians 11:1-30**

Paul addresses cultural and spiritual issues concerning differences between women and men in the first part of Chapter 11.

Nevertheless, neither is man independent of woman, nor woman independent of man, in the Lord. For woman came from man, even so man also comes through woman; but all things are from God.
—1 Corinthians 11:11-12

How do I appreciate, respect, and honor both men and women in their differences?

_____

_____

_____

The communion table brings both men and women together as they share in the Lord's brokenness and their own (verse 20-34).

But let a man examine himself... For he who eats and drinks in an unworthy manner eats and drinks judgment to himself, not discerning the Lord's body.
—1 Corinthians 11:28-29

If I do not examine myself, judge myself, and confess unresolved sin before taking communion:

❑ I bring judgment on myself (verse 29)

❑ I may get weak, sick, or even die (verse 30)

How will I prepare myself before taking communion?

_____

_____

_____

_____

Day 24: **1 Corinthians 11:31-12:3**

For if we would judge ourselves, we would not be judged. But when we are judged, we are chastened by the Lord, that we may not be condemned with the world.

—1 Corinthians 11:31-32

How is my relationship with Jesus impacted by knowing that I will not be condemned with the world when I judge myself and allow the Lord to discipline me?

_____

_____

_____

...[N]o one speaking by the Spirit of God calls Jesus accursed, and no one can say that Jesus is Lord except by the Holy Spirit.
—1 Corinthians 12:3

What are words that come out of my mouth indicating I am full of the Holy Spirit? What words come out of my mouth that are not of the Holy Spirit?

_____

_____

_____

How do I speak about Jesus to everyone?

_____

_____

_____

_____

Day 25: **1 Corinthians 12:1-7**

Now concerning spiritual gifts...

—1 Corinthians 12:1

❑ There are diversities of gifts, but the same Spirit (verse 4)

❑ There are differences of ministries, but the same Lord (verse 5)

❑ And there are diversities of activities, but it is the same God who works all in all (verse 6)

But the manifestation of the Spirit is given to each one for the profit of all.

—1 Corinthians 12:7

How am I profiting others through the gifts the Spirit has given me?

_____

_____

_____

_____

How am I profiting others by the ministry I am called to do?

_____

_____

_____

How am I profiting others through the activities of my daily life?

_____

_____

_____

_____

Day 26: **1 Corinthians 12:8-10**

Here are some of the gifts of the Holy Spirit:

- ❑ The word of wisdom (verse 8)

- ❑ The word of knowledge (verse 8)

- ❑ Faith (verse 9)

- ❑ The gifts of healing (verse 9)

- ❑ The working of miracles (verse 10)

- ❑ Prophecy (verse 10)

- ❑ Discernment of spirits (verse 10)

- ❑ Different kinds of tongues (verse 10)

- ❑ The interpretation of tongues (verse 10)

Do I recognize my gifts from the list above? If I do not, how will I pray the Lord brings clarification?

_____

_____

_____

_____

_____

What would be my ultimate hope for being able to use my gifts?

_____

_____

_____

_____

_____

Day 27: 1 Corinthians 12:8-26

But one and the same Spirit works all these things, distributing to each one individually as He wills.

—1 Corinthians 12:11

For as the body is one and has many members...

—1 Corinthians 12:12

For by one Spirit we were all baptized into one body... and have all been made to drink into one Spirit.

—1 Corinthians 12:13

But now God has set the members, each one of them, in the body just as He pleased.

—1 Corinthians 12:18

But now indeed there are many members, yet one body.

—1 Corinthians 12:20

...[B]ut God composed the body, having given greater honor to that part which lacks it, that there should be no schism in the body, but that the members should have the same care for one another.

—1 Corinthians 12:24-25

And if one member suffers, all the members suffer with it; or if one member is honored, all the members rejoice with it.

—1 Corinthians 12:26

When it comes to operating in the body of believers, how do I respond when others do not function in the way I do or see things the way I see them?

_____

_____

_____

_____

_____

_____

Day 28: 1 Corinthians 12:27-30

Now you are the body of Christ, and members individually.
—1 Corinthians 12:27

How much am I longing to be an important and significant part of the body of Christ?

< 1 – 2 – 3 – 4 – 5 – 6 – 7 – 8 – 9 – 10 > (circle one and explain)

_____

_____

_____

These are appointed by God in the church (verse 28):

- ❑ First apostles (verse 28)

- ❑ Second prophets (verse 28)

- ❑ Third teachers (verse 28)

- ❑ Next miracles (verse 28)

- ❑ Then gifts of healings, helps, administrations, varieties of tongues (verse 28)

How do I identify and use my gifts in the church?

_____

_____

_____

How do I support and encourage my brothers and sisters in Christ to walk in their spiritual gifts?

_____

_____

_____

Day 29: 1 Corinthians 12: 31-13:13

But earnestly desire the best gifts. And yet I show you a more excellent way.
—1 Corinthians 12:31

Though I speak with the tongues of men and of angels, but have not love, I have become sounding brass or a clanging cymbal.
—1 Corinthians 13:1

And though I have the gift of prophecy, and understand all mysteries and all knowledge, and though I have all faith, so that I could remove mountains, but have not love, I am nothing.
—1 Corinthians 13:2

And though I bestow all my goods to feed the poor, and though I give my body to be burned, but have not love, it profits me nothing.
—1 Corinthians 13:3

Love never fails. But whether there are prophecies, they will fail; whether there are tongues, they will cease; whether there is knowledge, it will vanish away.
—1 Corinthians 13:8

And now abide faith, hope, love... the greatest is love.
—1 Corinthians 13:13

If I choose love above all things, what will I need to change?

_____

_____

_____

How do I operate in love without desiring greater acknowledgment from my gifts, faith, and/or sacrifices?

_____

_____

_____

Day 30: **1 Corinthians 13:4-7**

How I am doing in each of these areas?

LOVE:

❑ Suffers long (verse 4)

< 1 – 2 – 3 – 4 – 5 – 6 – 7 – 8 – 9 – 10 > (circle one and explain)

_____

_____

_____

_____

❑ Is kind (verse 4)

< 1 – 2 – 3 – 4 – 5 – 6 – 7 – 8 – 9 – 10 > (circle one and explain)

_____

_____

_____

_____

❑ Does not envy (verse 4)

< 1 – 2 – 3 – 4 – 5 – 6 – 7 – 8 – 9 – 10 > (circle one and explain)

_____

_____

_____

_____

_____

_____

Day 31: **1 Corinthians 13:4-7**

How I am doing in each of these areas?

LOVE:

❑ Does not parade itself, is not puffed up (verse 4)

< 1 – 2 – 3 – 4 – 5 – 6 – 7 – 8 – 9 – 10 > (circle one and explain)

_____

_____

_____

❑ Does not behave rudely (verse 5)

< 1 – 2 – 3 – 4 – 5 – 6 – 7 – 8 – 9 – 10 > (circle one and explain)

_____

_____

_____

❑ Does not seek its own (verse 5)

< 1 – 2 – 3 – 4 – 5 – 6 – 7 – 8 – 9 – 10 > (circle one and explain)

_____

_____

_____

❑ Is not provoked (verse 5)

< 1 – 2 – 3 – 4 – 5 – 6 – 7 – 8 – 9 – 10 > (circle one and explain)

_____

_____

_____

Day 32: **1 Corinthians 13:4-7**

How I am doing in each of these areas?

LOVE:

❑ Thinks no evil (verse 5)

< 1 – 2 – 3 – 4 – 5 – 6 – 7 – 8 – 9 – 10 > (circle one and explain)

_____

_____

_____

_____

❑ Does not rejoice in iniquity (verse 6)

< 1 – 2 – 3 – 4 – 5 – 6 – 7 – 8 – 9 – 10 > (circle one and explain)

_____

_____

_____

_____

❑ Rejoices in truth (verse 6)

< 1 – 2 – 3 – 4 – 5 – 6 – 7 – 8 – 9 – 10 > (circle one and explain)

_____

_____

_____

_____

_____

_____

Day 33: **1 Corinthians 13:4-7**

How I am doing in each of these areas?

LOVE:

❑ Bears all things (verse 7)

< 1 – 2 – 3 – 4 – 5 – 6 – 7 – 8 – 9 – 10 > (circle one and explain)

_____

_____

_____

❑ Believes all things (verse 7)

< 1 – 2 – 3 – 4 – 5 – 6 – 7 – 8 – 9 – 10 > (circle one and explain)

_____

_____

_____

❑ Hopes all things (verse 7)

< 1 – 2 – 3 – 4 – 5 – 6 – 7 – 8 – 9 – 10 > (circle one and explain)

_____

_____

_____

❑ Endures all things (verse 7)

< 1 – 2 – 3 – 4 – 5 – 6 – 7 – 8 – 9 – 10 > (circle one and explain)

_____

_____

_____

Day 34: **1 Corinthians 14:1-31**

Pursue love, and desire spiritual gifts, but especially that you may prophesy.

—1 Corinthians 14:1

Prophesying:

- ❑ Means people can understand your language (verse 2)

- ❑ Edifies the church (verse 3, 4)

- ❑ Speaks exhortation (verse 3)

- ❑ Brings comfort (verse 3)

- ❑ It is for the believer (verse 22)

- ❑ It is for helping the unbeliever draw near and worship God that they may recognize God is in the midst of believers (verse 25)

- ❑ Is for the purpose of learning and encouragement (verse 31)

As I pursue love and spiritual gifts, how does prophesying fit into the things God has called me to do on behalf of the body of Christ?

_____

_____

_____

_____

Where is my passion level for building up the body of Christ?

< 1 – 2 – 3 – 4 – 5 – 6 – 7 – 8 – 9 – 10 > (circle one and explain)

_____

_____

_____

_____

Day 35: **1 Corinthians 14:2-40**

For he who speaks in a tongue does not speak to men but to God, for no one understands him; however, in the spirit he speaks mysteries.

—1 Corinthians 14:2

Here is what this passage says about speaking in tongues:

- ❏ They are speaking to God (verse 2)

- ❏ No one understands them (verse 2)

- ❏ They are speaking mysteries in the spirit (verse 2)

- ❏ It edifies the one who is speaking (verse 4)

- ❏ It does not profit the body of Christ (verse 6)

- ❏ Tongues need prayer for interpretation (verse 13)

- ❏ Singing in the Spirit needs interpretation (verse 15)

- ❏ No one can be in agreement without understanding (verse 16)

- ❏ Is a sign for the unbeliever (verse 22)

- ❏ At the most two or three are to speak in turn, with interpretation (verse 27)

- ❏ If no one interprets the tongue spoken, the person who spoke needs to be silent in the church (verse 28)

What kind of teaching and experience have I had concerning the gifts of tongues? How does it line up with these scriptures?

_____

_____

_____

_____

Day 36: **1 Corinthians 14:5-40**

I wish you all spoke with tongues, but even more that you prophesied; for he who prophesies is greater than he who speaks with tongues, unless indeed he interprets, that the church may receive edification.

—1 Corinthians 14:5

Since the Bible gives importance to the role in the body of Christ regarding prophesying and the interpretation of tongues, how will I pray about these gifts for myself and the church?

_____

_____

_____

For God is not the author of confusion but of peace, as in all the churches of the saints.

—1 Corinthians 14:33

Let all things be done decently and in order.

—1 Corinthians 14:40

Part of the litmus test for the true church:

❑ No confusion (verse 33)

❑ Peaceful (verse 33)

❑ Things are done in a decent way (verse 40)

❑ Things are in order (verse 40)

What does it mean to me to attend or belong to a church where these elements occur in some way?

_____

_____

_____

_____

Day 37: 1 Corinthians 15:1-10

Paul addresses brethren describing what happened when he declared the gospel to them (verse 1):

❑ They received the gospel (verse 1)

❑ They stood strong in the gospel (verse 1)

He goes onto say they were saved:

❑ Because they held fast to the word which he preached to them (verse 2)

How does this message of being saved challenge me?

_____

_____

_____

Paul then gives his testimony and shares the gospel of Jesus' death for our sins, His resurrection, and gives an account of everyone who saw Christ when He rose from the dead.
(verses 3-7)

Paul says he saw Jesus before he followed Christ (verse 8).

For I am the least of the apostles, who am not worthy to be called an apostle, because I persecuted the church of God.

—1 Corinthians 15:9

But by the grace of God I am what I am….

—1 Corinthians 15:10

How has the grace of God made me who and what I am?

_____

_____

_____

_____

Day 38: 1 Corinthians 15:11-32

Believing Christ raised from the dead is essential (verse 12-19).

But if there is no resurrection of the dead, then Christ is not risen. [T]hen... your faith is empty... [y]ou are still in your sins!
—1 Corinthians 15:13-14, 17

But now Christ is risen from the dead....
—1 Corinthians 15:20

...[I]n Christ all shall be made alive... who are Christ's at His coming.
—1 Corinthians 15:22-23

How does the resurrection power of Jesus make me full of faith?

_____

_____

_____

_____

_____

Then comes the end, when He delivers the kingdom to God the Father, when He puts an end to all rule and all authority and power. The last enemy that will be destroyed is death.
—1 Corinthians 15:24, 26

Does this news excite me or frighten me? How am I preparing for the end?

_____

_____

_____

_____

_____

_____

Day 39: **1 Corinthians 15:33-56**

Do not be deceived: "Evil company corrupts good habits."

—1 Corinthians 15:33

Without blaming others, how do I stay in the company of those who promote good habits?

_____

_____

_____

Awake to righteousness, and do not sin….

—1 Corinthians 15:34

How do I awaken to righteousness in areas of my life where I am tempted to sin?

_____

_____

_____

…[W]hat you sow is not made alive unless it dies.

—1 Corinthians 15:36

So also is the resurrection of the dead. The body is sown in corruption, it is raised in incorruption. It is sown in dishonor, it is raised in glory. It is sown in weakness, it is raised in power. It is sown a natural body, it is raised a spiritual body….

—1 Corinthians 15:42-44

In what area of corruption, dishonor, or weakness in my natural body am I most looking forward experiencing resurrection?

_____

_____

_____

_____

Day 40: **1 Corinthians 15:57-58**

But thanks be to God, who gives us the victory through our Lord Jesus Christ.

—1 Corinthians 15:57

Therefore, my beloved brethren...

—1 Corinthians 15:58

❑ Be steadfast (verse 58)

❑ Be immovable (verse 58)

❑ Be always abounding in the work of the Lord (verse 58)

❑ Know your labor is not in vain in the Lord (verse 58)

Since Christ gives me the victory through Jesus, how does that help me to be steadfast?

_____

Since Christ gives me the victory through Jesus, how does that help me to be immovable?

_____

_____

Since Christ gives me the victory through Jesus, how does that help me to be always abounding in the work of the Lord?

_____

_____

Since Christ gives me the victory through Jesus, how does that help me to know my labor for Him is not in vain?

_____

_____

_____

Day 41: **1 Corinthians 16:1-24**

This chapter reveals Paul's intimate and honest relationship with the believers at Corinth. Paul is straightforward in what he tells them, shares with them, and asks of them.

Here are some examples:

And it may be that I will remain, or even spend the winter with you, that you may send me on my journey, wherever I go.

—1 Corinthians 16:6

For I do not wish to see you now on the way; but I hope to stay a while with you, if the Lord permits.

—1 Corinthians 16:7

And if Timothy comes, see that he may be with you without fear….

—1 Corinthians 16:10

I urge you, brethren… submit… to everyone who works and labors with us.

—1 Corinthians 16:15-16

I am glad about the coming of Stephanas, Forunatus, and Achaicus, for what was lacking on your part they supplied. For they refreshed my spirit and yours. Therefore acknowledge such men.

—1 Corinthians 16:17-18

The churches of Asia greet you… Greet one another with a holy kiss.

—1 Corinthians 16:19-20

Am I moved or drawn to this kind of relationship among the body of believers? If not, why? If so, how am I moved or drawn?

_____

_____

_____

_____

Day 42: **1 Corinthians 16:14-24**

Let all that you do be done with love.

—1 Corinthians 16:14

What will it take for me to get to the place where whatever I do is done with love?

_____

_____

_____

_____

_____

If anyone does not love the Lord Jesus Christ, let him be accursed, O Lord, come!

—1 Corinthians 16:22

Where is my love for Jesus on this scale?

< 1 – 2 – 3 – 4 – 5 – 6 – 7 – 8 – 9 – 10 > (circle one and explain)

_____

_____

_____

How do I determine I have love for Jesus? What will it take to love Him more?

_____

_____

_____

_____

A

NEW TESTAMENT

28 Days
In
II CORINTHIANS

Day 1: **2 Corinthians 1:1-7**

Blessed be the God and Father of our Lord Jesus Christ, the Father of mercies and God of all comfort, who comforts us all in our tribulation, that we may be able to comfort those who are in any trouble, with the comfort with which we ourselves are comforted by God. For as the sufferings of Christ abound in us, so our consolation also abounds through Christ.

—2 Corinthians 1:3-5

What kind of comfort have I received from God?

_____

_____

How have I comforted others with understanding out of my own suffering?

_____

_____

How have I experienced receiving comfort from people who understood my suffering?

_____

_____

_____

Notice that the passage is referring to the sufferings of Christ. What kind of suffering have I experienced that would be considered the sufferings of Christ? Or, what examples of people in my life have had this kind of suffering?

_____

_____

_____

Day 2: **2 Corinthians 1:8-11**

Paul describes his sufferings for Christ:

❑ We were burdened beyond measure (verse 8)

❑ We were burdened beyond strength (verse 8)

❑ We despaired even of life (verse 8)

❑ We had the sentence of death in ourselves (verse 9)

Have I ever been able to relate to any of these? How did I gain comfort?

_____

_____

_____

The sufferings described in verses 8- 9 helped Paul and his companions to learn:

❑ We should not trust in ourselves but in God who raises the dead (verse 9)

❑ God delivered us from death (verse 10)

❑ God delivers us (verse 10)

❑ We trust He will continue to deliver us (verse 11)

❑ We are helped by prayers (verse 11)

How am I able to relate, or not relate, to these verses?

_____

_____

_____

_____

Day 3: **2 Corinthians 1:12-24**

Through all of Paul and his companion's sufferings their conduct testified to the world:

❑ Simplicity and godly sincerity (verse 12)

❑ Godly wisdom (verse 12)

❑ Conducting themselves by the grace of God (verse 12)

❑ Conducting themselves abundantly towards those who prayed for them and supported them (verse 12)

What kind of testimony do I desire to leave to those around me when I suffer? How does it compare to verse 12?

_____

_____

_____

Paul's word to the Corinthians is straightforward and honest (verse 17-19).

For all the promises of God in Him are Yes, and in Him Amen to the glory of God through us.

—2 Corinthians 1:20

❑ I am established and anointed by God (verse 21)

❑ I am sealed; my heart is full of the Holy Spirit (verse 22)

❑ By faith I stand (verse 24)

Since I have all of God available to me because of Jesus, how am I walking in Him according to this list?

_____

_____

_____

Day 4: 2 Corinthians 2:1-14

In verses 1-10 Paul demonstrates his love and care for the church of God in Corinth. He urges love and forgiveness towards those who cause grief.

He states the importance to forgive in the presence of Christ (verse 10):

...lest Satan should take advantage of us; for we are not ignorant of his devices.

—2 Corinthians 2:11

One of Satan's devices to take advantage of me is allowing unforgiveness in my life. Is there anyone I need to forgive? How difficult is it for me to forgive and not be offended by others?

_____

_____

_____

_____

_____

Now thanks be to God who always leads us in triumph in Christ....

—2 Corinthians 2:14

How am I always being led in triumph by Christ?

_____

_____

_____

_____

_____

_____

Day 5: 2 Corinthians 2:14-17

Because we are led in triumph, we have the aroma of God. These are the results of the aroma of God in us (verses 14-16):

❑ It diffuses the fragrance of His knowledge in every place through us (verse 14)

❑ We are the fragrance of Christ among those who are being saved (verse 15)

❑ We are the fragrance of Christ among those who are perishing (verse 15)

❑ Among those who are perishing we are the aroma of death (verse 16)

❑ Among those being saved we are the aroma of life (verse 16)

❑ We sincerely speak on behalf of Jesus in the sight of God (verses 16-17)

Since having the aroma of God is in connection to being led in triumph through Christ, where is my aroma level today?

< 1 – 2 – 3 – 4 – 5 – 6 – 7 – 8 – 9 – 10 > (circle one and explain)

_____

_____

_____

_____

How will the awareness of having the aroma of God impact my day?

_____

_____

_____

_____

Day 6: 2 Corinthians 3:1-18

Paul gives his example of how ministry takes place through the Spirit of God in the hearts of God's people, emphasizing the difference between the law "written with ink" and the epistle of Christ written by the Spirit on tablets of the heart (verse 1-4).

Not that we are sufficient of ourselves to think of anything as being from ourselves, but our sufficiency is from God, who also made us sufficient as ministers of the new covenant, not of the letter but of the Spirit, for the letter kills, but the Spirit gives life.

—2 Corinthians 3:5-6

How has the Spirit of God given me life and made me sufficient to minister to others?

_____

_____

_____

Paul tells of the glory of the commandments in the Old Testament. The children of Israel could not look at the glory because their minds were blinded (verses 7-14).

But even to this day, when Moses is read, a veil lies on their heart. Nevertheless when one turns to the Lord, the veil is taken away. Now the Lord is the Spirit; and where the Spirit of the Lord is, there is liberty.

—2 Corinthians 3:15-17

Since there is freedom where the Spirit of the Lord is, how would I describe my freedom in the Lord today? How do I need to pray today?

_____

_____

_____

_____

Day 7: **2 Corinthians 4:1-6**

For we do not preach ourselves, but Christ Jesus the Lord... For it is the God who commanded light to shine out of darkness, who has shone in our hearts to give the light of the knowledge of the glory of God in the face of Jesus Christ.

—2 Corinthians 4:5-6

We have the ministry and glory of God displayed in and through us because of God's mercy, which gives us strength to not lose heart (verse 1).

The glory of God in us helps us to:

- ❑ Renounce the hidden things of shame (verse 2)

- ❑ Not walk in craftiness (verse 2)

- ❑ Not handle the word of God deceitfully (verse 2)

- ❑ Clearly show the truth (verse 2)

- ❑ Be trustworthy to every person (verse 2)

How am I walking and ministering to others in these ways?

_____

_____

_____

How is the light of the knowledge of God's glory changing me as I focus on Jesus?

_____

_____

_____

_____

_____

Day 8: **2 Corinthians 4:7-18**

*Following Jesus is costly but holds eternal promises. A Christian has
hope as modeled by Paul and his companions.*

- ❏ We are hard-pressed on every side, yet not crushed (verse 8)

- ❏ We are perplexed, but not in despair (verse 8)

- ❏ We are persecuted, but not forsaken (verse 9)

- ❏ We are struck down, but not destroyed (verse 9)

*What costs have I experienced in following Jesus? Am I able to
relate to anything Paul describes above?*

_____

_____

_____

_____

_____

**...[K]nowing that He who raised up the Lord Jesus will also raise us
up with Jesus... Therefore do not lose heart. Even though our
outward man is perishing, yet the inward man is being renewed
day by day. For the things which are seen are temporary, but the
things which are not seen are eternal.**

—2 Corinthians 4:14,16,18

What temporary things challenge my eternal view?

_____

_____

_____

_____

_____

Day 9: **2 Corinthians 5:1-11**

For we know that if our earthly house, this tent, is destroyed, we have a building from God, a house not made with hands, eternal in the heavens.

—2 Corinthians 5:1

With the promise of eternal life in heaven:

- ❑ We desire to be clothed with our habitation from heaven (verse 2)

- ❑ Mortality will be swallowed up by life (verse 4)

- ❑ God has prepared us for this new life (verse 5)

- ❑ The Holy Spirit is our guarantee for immortality and life with Him (verse 5)

- ❑ We walk by faith and not by what we see around us (verse 7)

- ❑ We will appear before the judgment seat of Christ (verse 10)

- ❑ We will receive according to the good or bad we have done (verse 10)

- ❑ Knowing the terror of the Lord, we persuade people to know Christ (verse 11)

Which of these challenge me the most and why?

_____

_____

_____

Which of these are easy for me to hear and believe?

_____

_____

_____

Day 10: 2 Corinthians 5:12-21

Therefore, if anyone is in Christ, he is a new creation; old things have passed away; behold, all things have become new.
—2 Corinthians 5:17

What specifically has God made new in me that is significantly different from the old me?

_____

_____

_____

_____

This is what God has done for me:

- ❑ He reconciled me to Himself through Jesus Christ (verse 18)

- ❑ He gave me the ministry of reconciliation and the word of reconciliation through Jesus Christ (verse 18)

- ❑ He made Jesus—who knew no sin—to become sin for me (verse 21)

This is what I will do for Him:

- ❑ I am an ambassador of Christ to implore others to be reconciled to God through Jesus (verse 20)

- ❑ I am the righteousness of God in Christ Jesus (verse 21)

As an ambassador of Christ with the ministry of reconciliation, how will I implore others to be reconciled to Jesus?

_____

_____

_____

_____

Day 11: 2 Corinthians 6:1-4

We then, as workers together with Him… We give no offense in anything, that our ministry may not be blamed.
—2 Corinthians 6:1, 3

How do I work with Jesus?

_____

_____

How do I keep from offending others?

_____

_____

But in all things we commend ourselves as ministers of God…
—2 Corinthians 6:4

How am I doing in each area of these as I work alongside God?

❑ In much patience (verse 4)

< 1 – 2 – 3 – 4 – 5 – 6 – 7 – 8 – 9 – 10 > (circle one and explain)

_____

_____

❑ In tribulation and distress (verse 4)

< 1 – 2 – 3 – 4 – 5 – 6 – 7 – 8 – 9 – 10 > (circle one and explain)

_____

_____

❑ In needs (verse 4)

< 1 – 2 – 3 – 4 – 5 – 6 – 7 – 8 – 9 – 10 > (circle one and explain)

_____

_____

Day 12: **2 Corinthians 6:4-7**

But in all things we commend ourselves as ministers of God... [I]n stripes, in imprisonments, in tumults, in labors, in sleeplessness, in fastings....

—2 Corinthians 6:4-5

Paul faced some things I may never face. How am I preparing to face the things listed above in case of persecution?

_____

_____

_____

These empower a minister of God to help face trials of every type:

- ❑ Purity (verse 6)
- ❑ Knowledge (verse 6)
- ❑ Longsuffering (verse 6)
- ❑ Kindness (verse 6)
- ❑ The Holy Spirit (verse 6)
- ❑ Sincere Love (verse 6)
- ❑ The Word of Truth (verse 7)
- ❑ The Power of God (verse 7)
- ❑ The Armor of Righteousness (verse 7)

How have these empowered me to minister to others and to face trials?

_____

_____

_____

_____

Day 13: 2 Corinthians 6:8-10

Paul continues describing all he and his companions have faced as workers of God.

[B]y honor and dishonor, by evil report and good report; as deceivers, and yet true; as unknown, and yet well known; as dying, and behold we live; as chastened, and yet not killed; as sorrowful, yet always rejoicing; as poor, yet making many rich; as having nothing, and yet possessing all things.

—2 Corinthians 6:8-10

How emotionally stable am I to face all these types of contradictions in my life?

< 1 – 2 – 3 – 4 – 5 – 6 – 7 – 8 – 9 – 10 > (circle one and explain)

_____

_____

_____

_____

_____

What is my confidence level in believing the Lord will pull through for me no matter how good or bad things get?

< 1 – 2 – 3 – 4 – 5 – 6 – 7 – 8 – 9 – 10 > (circle one and explain)

_____

_____

_____

_____

_____

_____

Day 14: **2 Corinthians 6:11-18**

Paul describes the kind of open communication he desires with believers.

…We have spoken openly to you, our heart is wide open. You are not restricted by us, but you are restricted by your own affections. Now in return for the same… you also be open.

—2 Corinthians 6:11-13

What personal restrictions limit my own affections and impact my openness to other believers?

_____

_____

_____

_____

Do not be unequally yoked together with unbelievers.

**For what fellowship has righteousness with lawlessness?
And what communion has light with darkness?
And what accord has Christ with Belial [Satan]?
Or what part has a believer with an unbeliever?
And what agreement has the temple of God with idols?**

For you are the temple of the living God….

—2 Corinthians 6:14-16

Since knowing Christ as Savior, have I ever been tied closely to unbelievers? If so, what influence did this have on me?

_____

_____

_____

_____

Day 15: **2 Corinthians 7:1-16**

Therefore, having these promises, beloved, let us cleanse ourselves from all filthiness of the flesh and spirit, perfecting holiness in the fear of God.

—2 Corinthians 7:1

Because perfecting holiness and cleansing of my flesh and spirit can only come through repentance and Jesus' shed blood on the cross, how will I proceed according to this verse?

_____

_____

_____

Paul says those in the church at Corinth can open their hearts to him and those ministering with him (verse 2).

Here are a few reasons he gives:

- ❑ We have wronged no one (verse 2)
- ❑ We have corrupted no one (verse 2)
- ❑ We have cheated no one (verse 2)
- ❑ We have you in our hearts (verse 3)
- ❑ I boast about you (verse 3)
- ❑ I have confidence in you (verse 16)

What has my experience been in giving and receiving this kind of care among believers?

_____

_____

_____

_____

Day 16: **2 Corinthians 7:4-11**

...God, who comforts the downcast...
—2 Corinthians 7:6

Paul explains his great love and joyful suffering for the believers at Corinth. He also appreciates their zeal for him. Although Paul's letter made them sorrowful for a little while, it brought about a good outcome (verses 4-8).

Paul reminds them what came out of godly sorrow:

- ❑ They received God's comfort (verse 6)

- ❑ It led them to repentance (verse 9)

- ❑ It produced diligence (verse 11)

- ❑ They were cleared from blame (verse 11)

For godly sorrow produces repentance leading to salvation...
—2 Corinthians 7:10

...[T]he sorrow of this world produces death.
—2 Corinthians 710

Compared to the things mentioned in the above verses how have sorrow and grief impacted my life?

_____

_____

_____

_____

_____

_____

_____

Day 17: **2 Corinthians 8:1-7**

God's grace to the Macedonian churches looked like this (verse 1):

❑ The people were abundant in joy (verse 2)

❑ The people were abundant in godly riches (verse 2)

❑ Affliction and poverty were not obstacles as the people served the body of Christ (verse 2-4)

❑ They gave themselves to the Lord first, then to others (verse 5)

How hungry am I for the things that come from God's grace?

< 1 – 2 – 3 – 4 – 5 – 6 – 7 – 8 – 9 – 10 > (circle one and explain)

_____

_____

_____

Not only had God graced the church, but the coming of Titus would also minister grace. Paul encouraged the believers to abound in the grace Titus would bring (verse 6-7).

Paul also encouraged them to abound:

❑ In faith (verse 7)

❑ In speech (verse 7)

❑ In knowledge (verse 7)

❑ In all diligence (verse 7)

❑ In love (verse 7)

In which areas am I abounding? In which areas am I lacking?

_____

_____

_____

Day 18: 2 Corinthians 8:8-24

And this I give advice: It is to your advantage not only to be doing what you began and were desiring to do a year ago; but now you also must complete the doing of it; that as there was a readiness to desire it, so there also may be a completion out of what you have. For if there is first a willing mind, it is accepted according to what one has, and not according to what he does not have.

—2 Corinthians 8:10-12

What is stirring in me that God has called me to do and is not yet complete?

_____

_____

_____

_____

_____

For I do not mean that others should be eased and you burdened; but by an equality, that now at this time your abundance may supply their lack, that their abundance also may supply your lack— that there may be equality.

—2 Corinthians 8:13-14

How does this kind of fellowship pull on my heart? When in my life have I experienced believers of Jesus functioning in this manner?

_____

_____

_____

_____

_____

_____

Day 19: **2 Corinthians 9:1-8**

...He who sows sparingly will also reap sparingly, and he who sows bountifully will also reap bountifully.
—2 Corinthians 9:6 (Proverbs 1:24, 22:9)

How would I measure the effort I put into sowing through my abilities?

< 1 – 2 – 3 – 4 – 5 – 6 – 7 – 8 – 9 – 10 > (circle one and explain)

_____

_____

_____

What areas of my life seem sparse?

_____

_____

What areas of my life am I currently reaping bountifully?

_____

_____

So let each one give as he purposes in his heart, not grudgingly or of necessity; for God loves a cheerful giver. And God is able to make all grace abound toward you, that you, always having all sufficiency in all things, may have an abundance for every good work.
—2 Corinthians 9:7-8

How would I measure my cheerfulness in giving for the work of the Lord?

< 1 – 2 – 3 – 4 – 5 – 6 – 7 – 8 – 9 – 10 > (circle one and explain)

_____

_____

_____

Day 20: **2 Corinthians 9:7-15**

Now may He who supplies seed to the sower, and bread for food, supply and multiply the seed you have sown and increase the fruits of your righteousness.

—2 Corinthians 9:10

Thanks be to God for His indescribable gift!

—2 Corinthians 9:15

Chapter 9 reveals the ways we may increase when we joyfully sow seeds given to us by the Lord.

The increase may come in these ways:

- ❑ A cheerful heart (verse 7)

- ❑ Grace abounding towards us (verse 8)

- ❑ Having sufficiency in all things (verse 8)

- ❑ An abundance for good work (verse 8)

- ❑ Enriched in giving (verse 10)

- ❑ Thanksgiving (verse 11)

- ❑ Confession to the gospel of Christ (verse 13)

In which of these areas am I experiencing an increase?

_____

_____

_____

In which of these areas do I need an increase?

_____

_____

_____

_____

Day 21: 2 Corinthians 10:1-6

For though we walk in the flesh, we do not war according to the flesh. For the weapons of our warfare are not carnal but mighty in God for pulling down strongholds, casting down arguments and every high thing that exalts itself against the knowledge of God, bringing every thought into captivity to the obedience of Christ, and being ready to punish all disobedience when your obedience is fulfilled.

—2 Corinthians 10:3-6

Walking in the Holy Spirit means:

- ❑ We do not fight our battles in fleshly ways (verse 3)

- ❑ The weapons we use to fight our battles are not carnal (verse 4)

- ❑ Our weapons are mighty in God for pulling down strongholds (verse 4)

- ❑ Our weapons cast down arguments (verse 5)

- ❑ Our weapons cast down every high thing that exalts itself against the knowledge of God (verse 5)

- ❑ Our weapons bring every thought into the obedience of Christ (verse 5)

- ❑ Our weapons punish all disobedience after we have been obedient (verse 6)

What battles am I fighting that need the use of these weapons?

_____

_____

_____

_____

_____

Day 22: 2 Corinthians 10:7-18

For we dare not class ourselves or compare ourselves with those who commend themselves. But they, measuring themselves by themselves, and comparing themselves among themselves, are not wise.

—2 Corinthians 10:12

How do I deal with peer pressure and people pleasing?

_____

_____

_____

_____

But "he who glories, let him glory in the Lord."

—2 Corinthians 10:17 (Jeremiah 9:24)

What are some ways in which I glory in the Lord?

_____

_____

_____

_____

For not he who commends himself is approved, but whom the Lord commends.

—2 Corinthians 10:18

When have I felt commended by the Lord?

_____

_____

_____

_____

Day 23: **2 Corinthians 11:1-10**

Paul is once again pleading with God's people to not be deceived.

But I fear, lest somehow, as the serpent deceived Eve by his craftiness, so your minds may be corrupted from the simplicity that is in Christ.

—2 Corinthians 11:3 (Genesis 3:4,13)

What thoughts do I have about the simplicity that is in Jesus?

_____

_____

_____

In what ways might I complicate the gospel of Jesus?

_____

_____

_____

...And in everything I [Paul] kept myself from being burdensome to you, and so I will keep myself. As the truth of Christ is in me, no one shall stop me from this boasting in the regions of Achaia. Why? Because I do not love you? God knows!

—2 Corinthians 11:9-11

Have I ever experienced someone's love and care for me extended purely for the sake of helping me stay focused on Jesus? If so, how did I respond?

_____

_____

_____

_____

Day 24: **2 Corinthians 11:11-15**

Paul declares there are false teachers trying to deceive by preaching another gospel other than what he has taught about Jesus (verses 4, 12).

For such are false apostles, deceitful workers, transforming themselves into apostles of Christ. And no wonder! For Satan himself transforms himself into an angel of light. Therefore it is no great thing if his ministers also transform themselves into ministers of righteousness, whose end will be according to their works.
—2 Corinthians 11:13-15

What methods and tools do I use to determine whether what I hear is false or true?

_____

_____

_____

_____

_____

_____

Since so many ministers preach a slightly different version of the gospel, how do I determine truth from false teaching?

_____

_____

_____

_____

_____

_____

Day 25: **2 Corinthians 11:16-33**

Paul shares in his letter what he has gone through to fulfill the calling God has laid on him (verses 16-33).

…[F]ive times I received forty stripes minus one. Three times I was beaten with rods; once I was stoned; three times I was shipwrecked; a night and a day I have been in the deep; in journeys often, in perils of waters, in perils of robbers, in perils of my own countrymen, in perils of the Gentiles, in perils in the city, in perils in the wilderness, in perils in the sea, in perils among false brethren; in weariness and toil, in sleeplessness often, in hunger and thirst, in fastings often, in cold and nakedness….

—2 Corinthians 11:24-27

With all Paul faced, this was his biggest concern:

…[W]hat comes upon me daily: my deep concern for all the churches.

—2 Corinthians 11:28

What are things God has called me to do daily for His sake?

_____

_____

_____

To what extent have I gone to fulfill my calling?

_____

_____

What can I do to extend myself further for the things I am called to fulfill for the sake of Jesus?

_____

_____

_____

Day 26: 2 Corinthians 12:1-9

For though I might desire to boast, I will not be a fool; for I will speak the truth. But I refrain, lest anyone should think of me above what he sees me to be or hears from me.

—2 Corinthians 12:6

How do my words and actions line up with what others think of me?

_____

_____

_____

And lest I should be exalted above measure by the abundance of the revelations, a thorn in the flesh was given to me, a messenger of Satan to buffet me, lest I be exalted above measure... I pleaded three times that it might depart from me.

—2 Corinthians 12:7-8

How have I been tempted to be arrogant about the things I know concerning the Lord and the revelations He has given me?

_____

_____

And He [Jesus] said to me, "My grace is sufficient for you, for My strength is made perfect in weakness."

—2 Corinthians 12:9

How does this verse speak to me?

_____

_____

_____

_____

_____

Day 27: 2 Corinthians 12:10-21

...[G]ladly I will rather boast in my infirmities, that the power of Christ may rest upon me. Therefore I take pleasure in infirmities, in reproaches, in needs, in persecutions, in distresses, for Christ's sake. For when I am weak, then I am strong.

—2 Corinthians 12:9-10

How does an area of weakness within me benefit my sharing the gospel of Jesus?

_____

_____

_____

Truly the signs of an apostle were accomplished among you...

—2 Corinthians 12:12

Here are the signs:

- ❑ All perseverance (verse 12)

- ❑ Signs and wonders (verse 12)

- ❑ Mighty deeds (verse 12)

How do I see the evidence of these things being accomplished in me and those around me?

_____

_____

_____

What have I been taught about walking in all perseverance, signs and wonders, and mighty deeds?

_____

_____

_____

Day 28: **2 Corinthians 13:1-14**

...Christ... is... mighty in you. For though He was crucified in weakness, yet He lives by the power of God. For we also are weak in Him, but we shall live with Him by the power of God toward you.
—2 Corinthians 13:3-4

How does understanding the power of God help me adjust my thinking about weaknesses?

_____

_____

...Do you not know... that Jesus Christ is in you?
—2 Corinthians 13:5

How would I answer this question?

_____

_____

The Lord gave Paul the authority to build up believers. He ends his letter with these encouraging words (verse 10):

- ❑ Be complete (verse 11)
- ❑ Be of good comfort (verse 11)
- ❑ Be of one mind (verse 11)
- ❑ Live in peace (verse 11)
- ❑ The God of love and peace will be with you (verse 11)

As I receive these words, what are my thoughts?

_____

_____

_____

Making Scripture Personal series
385 Days in Romans–Jude

Volume 1
- 40 Days in Romans
- 42 Days in 1 Corinthians
- 28 Days in 2 Corinthians

Volume 2
- 16 Days in Galatians
- 26 Days in Ephesians
- 11 Days in Philippians
- 17 Days in Colossians
- 12 Days in 1 Thessalonians
- 6 Days in 2 Thessalonians

Volume 3
- 22 Days in 1 Timothy
- 14 Days in 2 Timothy
- 14 Days in Titus/Philemon
- 45 Days in Hebrews

Volume 4
- 20 Days in James
- 24 Days in 1 Peter
- 16 Days in 2 Peter
- 21 Days in 1 2 3 John
- 11 Days in Jude

Making Scripture Personal Companion Journal 1 & 2
(for Volumes 1-2 and Volumes 3-4)

About the author

Anita K. Miller

The *Making Scripture Personal* series stems from Anita's lifelong passion to apply the scriptures in gaining freedom and answering life's many difficult questions.

Anita holds a Masters Degree in Counseling from Liberty University and a Bachelors Degree in Education. She is a Licensed Professional Counselor (MI).

She is the dedicated wife, mother, and grandmother and resides with her husband Timothy J Miller in Fort Wayne, Indiana.

Made in the USA
Columbia, SC
01 December 2021

49874781R00070